SKIN

SKIN

poems by

ROBERT VANDERMOLEN

MILKWEED EDITIONS

Published 2021 by Milkweed Editions
Printed in the United States
Cover design by Mary Austin Speaker
Cover photo/illustration by Beau Brashares / Millennium Images, UK
21 22 23 24 25 5 4 3 2 1
First Edition

Milkweed Editions, an independent nonprofit publisher, gratefully acknowledges sustaining support from our Board of Directors; the Alan B. Slifka Foundation and its president, Riva Ariella Ritvo-Slifka; the Amazon Literary Partnership; the Ballard Spahr Foundation; *Copper Nickel*; the McKnight Foundation; the National Endowment for the Arts; the National Poetry Series; the Target Foundation; and other generous contributions from foundations, corporations, and individuals. Also, this activity is made possible by the voters of Minnesota through a Minnesota State Arts Board Operating Support grant, thanks to a legislative appropriation from the arts and cultural heritage fund. For a full listing of Milkweed Editions supporters, please visit milkweed.org.

Library of Congress Control Number 2021930794

for Deb, Sean, and Colin

CONTENTS

THREE

SKIN

SCARLET TANAGER: 1967

An ice storm that snapped lines.
A surge of bravado
Music played too loud.
In winter when snow turned to pumice
I thought I'd leave. The lawn chair
I'd stolen I meant to return
To the tennis courts. Gracie ripped
All the pages from the books.
I pumped up the tires of the Ford
But couldn't decide where to travel.
At night: eleven lights
On the street. Sixteen cars and a motorcycle.
In the chill of privacy
One seeks promise—
I'd never heard turtles mating
For instance, or seen Walloon Lake
When trees were budding—
Which is how winter withered,
Writhed towards the stoops and steps.
Banisters and doors shrinking in sleep

ONE

TRAILS

It's relaxing here, the sense of here,
Except for train tracks
Hidden over the rise—
The freight that stumbles
Through before morning,
Like some misjudgment
From the evening before,
Something that rises up
Out of the murk of sleep and turns true

Wedges and edges of snow
Half-thawed, then frozen again

It was tough to walk
With equilibrium, even if one
Had a cane or shepherd's crook—
But I didn't comment

While sipping coffee
The sun glittering through pine
And cedar, it looked warmer.
It occurred to me, she continued,
One of those thoughts that slide
Into notice, like hunger—
You'll find this amusing, but I realized
I was never going to be a film director,
When I was with community theatre
I always figured it a possibility.
Like when Sean said (as a member
of the city commission),
No one goes into politics

Without a thought of becoming president:
Circumstances and chance,
Changing times, being able to look
Voters in the eye. And lie. I added that,
She said. We paused to glance
Into the black water of the stream

*

These afflicted shadows in the barn—
Imagined sounds sucked underground.
She peered at me pointedly

But I was hoping the barn was still sturdy
Though portions were missing.
A breeze pick up through
The windbreak outside

In battered weeds and drying snow
The carcass of a deer hit by a car
On 3 Mile Road.
Occasional brick and pipe rearing up

A large dimple of water in the pond

Sean, my ex, wasn't mean
Just thoughtless—you've no doubt
Heard this before. He grew self-absorbed,
Stopped heeding everyday events.
Inevitably he turned greyish
(or dim, I suppose), until it was difficult
To spot him in a room. I bought him
Red shirts. Changed the carpet.

But his voice dwindled
Until I had to move closer.
A day arrived when I didn't want
To drive home, regardless of the hour

Everything had become too solemn—
Like that barn with its cow stalls
And drains. Those gigantic wooden
Supports. It wasn't about fame or money,
Though I had some with modeling
(all of it fleeting, as it turned out).
The colors changed, like on a ball field
When the lights snap on or maybe
It was just the crowd stirring.
Then envision the reverse, dusk
On a shelf of ice up north past the bridge.
One does miss it for a time.
But I'm not fragile. It took me a while
To reorganize. I puttered about
Until I stumbled upon mosaics—

*

Corinne was rather tall. She was beaming now.
Her dark hair whipping back and forth
Along with red-wing blackbirds

INDOOR PLANTS

The street was wrapped in old prose.
Tedious weather brings on desire

That grazing look of Greer Garson
On the late movie, for instance

The clarity of evening
The talk of a Florida holiday

But everyone on hand determined
To be maladjusted

Winter conversation flops around like a flag
The color has gone out of

A book on Zen, another beer
Flipping through a catalog

Footfalls and a little cold air
Seeping in under the slider
On Saturday

Dead leaves on the carpet
Curling to resemble beetles

THE DAGGED EDGE

Wither back into yourself
He suggested. How far, you
Wondered? Back to a swarm
Of temblors? You merely wanted
To discuss the good ship Rita,
Traveling upriver into the final swamp,
Fruit bats and vultures.
Her angry melon face,
With lemons sliding across.
Actresses were larger then,
Men smaller. A captain leaning
With thoughts of his own
Under soiled clothes

She's taller than him, the woman
In her bulging two-piece.
It's also hot, you need a hat.
Hers has a hole. The scenery wiggles.
A woman scientist owning
A red mouth, waving generous arms,
In the morning she's alone.
The ship stuck in a round pond
Resembling a crater from
Dinosaur days. You recall this
From childhood. Then wake

THE CLOUDS

Startling sound
Of a hubcap crossing gravel

His skin like paper

*

Someone he once knew,
When he glanced from the menu,
Was striding across sand—
The sun squinting over water,
Cumulus like large potatoes
Buffeting above

*

The cottonwoods beginning
To rattle, the two of them
Sipping vodka in plastic cups

The circuits warming,
Clicking, as in a TV from childhood

Being anxious, the other says,
Keeps you alert—
Though the former was dissipating
Smartly. . .

Oily reek
From a closed concession stand

Swirl of hornets

As dusk is with airline lights
A sensation

EVENINGS & MORNINGS

There was something about the woman in the movie
As she sat in bed staring at the Smith & Wesson,
Allowing the sheet to slip to her waist. It was so
Unexpected. I was the guy with the gun
Making apologies I wouldn't have made before

*

The sun remaining dry, non-partisan
Across now the planks of September—
How difficult to piece one observation
Into the next without hyperbole or minor lie

Sometimes the lake has a bedroom smell.
No doubt, my neighbor replies, from our summer flooding. . .
Ropes frayed and green, while tame boats
Await storage—suddenly all the hidden birds
Commence their chirping and whining.
The water a Prussian blue.

A couple of crickets under the grill
The only thing covered in tension is you

LOWERING A SHOULDER

A cloud of dry snow
From hemlock boughs
Riding through air

And over ice, adoring ice
Of a beaver pond

Sound of a leaf skidding
Into deadfall—

The rapt attention
You can't find a source for—

As the ground tilts to the east
With massive indifference

*

It's peculiar how emptiness
Closes like a grey sheet

Origins lost
In some fundamental dusting
Of permanence

Science seems, when you think of it,
Too noisy, dandyish,
Said Uncle Jake, a veteran
Who'd fought in Burma

The two of us hunting hares
With .22s. A scent of mothballs
Rising from his sleeves,
Liquor from his breath—

*

Pausing at the muffled approach
Of a nameless creek, a cascade
Down limestone

This along a fault line
That hasn't budged for generations

NICK'S DREAM

I saw the senator
Sitting in front of his window,
Diane grown stout
In middle age
Leaning dimly behind him

I wondered too,
How much violence
Was merely threat,
Emptiness surrounding
A boiler, the piping, the clanging. . .

With her on the floor
Of the storeroom, I'm surprised
We weren't interrupted by staff.
No one came out of their rooms.
There weren't sounds
Of television either. . .

Past the circular gravel drive
I lit out across pastures
And woodlots. Perhaps I was in
Pennsylvania. . .

I wasn't thinking clearly

WOMAN READING

A democracy of winter light
On trees and brown ground

Cover terraces of snow melting
Over slopes, a time lag

For example before
The tug of remorse. The stream

And fish in shadow

I'm waiting for a phone call
Which could be demeaning

Or should I say rude? As wind
Tends to be after mild weather

It was a painting I was
Thinking of, something

Quiet from a century ago
A room without worry

More deep shades than now.
But it grew more fanciful

As I loitered near drapes
Like someone important

(but why be cheap?)
Like Lincoln, let's suggest,

During a spell of uncertain news,
Pondering his time perhaps

During the Black Hawk War.
Scent of rose water followed

By prunes. In the oaks
I thought I heard a frog

But it was a small woodpecker,
Grit dropping into snow

Small sounds distract me,
You understand. Nevertheless

I couldn't see or touch
The cover of her quarto

Pinching then
The ridge of his nose

My will has been sapped,
And who are these men

Nosing my trail
Through thicket and hardwood?

I had meant to ask him
About his '64 Buick on blocks

His hair was loose and white
Lingering below his shoulders

His boots, his cowboy clothes,
Were white as well

Oh hell, he declared

It's our weakness for splendor
In clouds and water

How the law and lawless
Keep changing sides

Inspiring days, we thought,
If we could maintain our stamina

COWBOYS AND COUPLES

Fisk Park has become part of the river
Part of an old arrangement

As in those doggerel westerns,
Two sets of hombres, pistols drawn

Who keep riding their ponies
Past the same outcroppings and knolls

Or with couples long used to each other. . .

You do ramble, she said, biting a corner
Of toast. Just say flood and be done with it

Happens every year. That's how big fish
Enter the pond. . .

That's what I meant, he suggested,
Smoothing his mustache with forefinger

And thumb. Like renewal? she asked,
I don't believe so, as she answered herself

After a moment,
More like monotony, the color of bark

BLACK LAKE

Two deer leaping up and down
In bulrushes, almost as if wondering
What I was doing after walleye season.
Of course nothing was biting along the drop-off.
Bored swans, and the sky as reddish
As midsummer. A frost worming south
Through hickory and sumac,
Old paths and broken bicycles. . .

An antique habit, sitting still,
Waiting for the poison to affect the senses
Let's say. With daydreams bulky,
Light fades from the strait between poplars
Where vines hang with small white flowers,
Less and less distinct

RAPTORS

I woke to southern gusts,
Mud cracking into pottery shards, last year's leaves
Racing like rats down the slope from the ridge

Eagles perched in almost every tree—
Replaced by hawks, then owls within days—
All slipping north into Canada on a wind made for fire

Next to the cabin I sat on a stump. The great birds,
Rocking under a milky sky, waited sober
In budding maple, eerily so—as porcupine and deer
Moseyed, scouting my two-track. I later found
My cap in a beaver pond, partly chewed. I seemed
To be irrelevant, as harmless as a scarecrow
Dripping straw

AFTER THE REUNION

So the dog wakes you
The neighbor's dog as well—
They were large Newfoundland warnings
Of a ship astray, men sweating in panic—
Raining with passion
Pieces of planking wading waves. . .

Next it was morning and sunny.
Strange, says your wife, sitting up
In the pale creases of light off water

The dog snoring like a sailor
The door unlatched, open

THE LAND

In his workshop
A silent noise of reflections
From glass and metal
His daughter saying, yes, everything needs work,
Cleaning up and clearing out—
Nick had made windmills for orchards
To combat frost. No frost this morning though
The calm pasture ripened down to mounds of aging clinkers
Above Mill Creek. I'd forgotten about clinkers.
We strolled and could hear steelhead thrashing
Up the slight rapids through a tangle of shrub elm
And box elder. Nick had looked old when he was young.
Then he didn't change much. My uncle's farm was down
The road where storage units now reside, row upon row,
Seen from a distance they look like barracks.
He was a John Bircher while Nick was anti-war.
Did you know my father well? We were in sports, I said.
There used to be workhorses here, I told her. This is where
They retired. I thought I saw smoke then I didn't.
My shoes were sopped with dew. She wore wellies
And reminded me again she was interested in selling
The half-section with small outbuildings, the faded barn,
The dark-slung house that resembled what you see
In rural Georgia surrounded by pecan trees. Here there
Are apricots. It's so confusing, she said, searching for advice,
Frowning, resembling her mother briefly,
A falcon streaking overhead under the steady
Warming of morning, a quiver crossing her lips. . .

INTERLUDE

I don't believe she married him
Because he was in the fish business
Remarked Lois, which quieted
The ensemble some

From upstairs, an old Leonard Cohen tune

It was unfortunate the attorney general was involved,
If at a distance

Lois was the sister of the AG
Her husband puffy and long on anecdotes
The banker at a bank that defaulted

In the spacious woodlot behind the house
Fireflies began to glitter
Then flying squirrels visiting bird feeders

A government vehicle sidled under a linden

He should have joined the Coast Guard
As his mother had wished

THE CRACK

There's a crack that runs through the island, she remarked,
From a balcony adjacent to ours. A fault line? I asked,
I don't think so, she said, a natural crack in the limestone,
That's what my grandfather told me. He grew up near
The crevasse, said people had been throwing refrigerators,
Stoves, broken tools, and so on into it for decades, maybe
Longer than that; the tour guides never discuss it.
We'll be taking a ferry over shortly, she explained, to look
At our properties. What would cause such a crack? No one
Knows, she said. I love your dog, she said. Have a good trip,
My wife said. Geese and mallards flew into the shallows,
And what appeared to be shadows turned out to be
Rotten pilings under clean water. The great hotel shimmered
White among trees below an escarpment. I'd be curious, I said,
How many other cracks are around here, the falls of the big river
On the other side of the bridge are on a fault, I know that.
Don't start, said my wife, we're on our second honeymoon,
We've got money from the sale of your mother's business,
Erin is doing fine at the university. How quiet it is, I said,
Before a boat horn sounded from one of the larger ferries,
Geese responding with honks. . .

LINCOLN LAKE

In March the ice, as we stood there,
Knifing away from shore,
Was a plate a mile long, half a foot thick

In August you put down your chicken,
Wiped your hands on a paper napkin,
Seated at a lawn table I'd painted red

Two swans beat through the air
Between the willows and you

AFTER THE FOG

Shaving:
If I had a thinner face
Like D. H. Lawrence
Or Robert Creeley
I'd grow a beard (I told her)

*

The yellows of winter sunsets
Over water, sliding into peach

*

Trash stuck in hedges
Like old carnations

*

There were odd sounds
Emanating from the dog
Lying next to the wall—
When I pried her mouth loose
A warbler flew out

SPRING AND ALL

A lisp of ocean air
Far from the coast

Like thought without substance

So many bartenders
Named Chris or Rick

I couldn't pick him out of a lineup
Wendy Pilling confessed

While Dick said
They found my college ID

Missing for twenty years

At the scene of the kidnapping
On Ariana Street—

I said, are you people crazy

*

A snow fence
Half its teeth missing

Bordering the sand of Perch Lake
At the sunny end of Prospect

Where the marina operators
Haven't returned

From Florida. Marcus
Pulled on a Marlboro

Declared, I'll never vote
For a Christian again

And Mrs. Cato ruminated:
I loved him for six months

When he was twenty (he told me),
I was thirty-two—

I didn't understand he was younger

Randy Smits scratched his chin
Spit at a nugget of asphalt in sand

*

After all, Martin Luther
Enjoyed his beer

Crunched cans. Whine of the yellow
Ambulance

Big John Rabideau was the sheriff
Then

He punched me once in the kidneys

Marcus bent to tie a shoelace

Wendy Pilling rolled her eyes

*

After a poor night of sleep
I forgot everything I had left to do

Said Colin.
Some people idealize

Their situations. Not me.
Victorian hearts reverberating

In the wrought-iron railing,
Some up, some down

An older woman leaves the house
Pulling a black terrier on a leash

Unlocks the gate. A kind of false hope
Said Dick

*

Daffodils,
A double line down the center

Of the boulevard
Leading back to the courthouse

To which all roads lead

MILES DAVIS

That period before visitors
When the light hums overhead

You dissolve
With no one to answer to.

An hour, a day, a week.
The light, the door. . .

Tailing off. Just as it
Should be.

Except that nothing is the same
Or exactly true.

What visitors
Are we talking about?

ON TUESDAY

Spotting a van logging

Through beeches, where you hadn't
Realized there was a road

Staring from your canoe, water lilies
And heron, stumps on the bottom

A murderous quiet
The surface of the lake like skin

*

Well, she did look a little
Like Mia Farrow, though taller,

Seated by her current boyfriend
Beneath a yellow overhang

The sky dim as old Plexiglas

*

It's tough to remain focused while
Uneasy. The models appearing

Under-aged in the wrinkled magazines
You notice while buying rum in the party store

The men on stools, farmers, seem to
Have been sitting there for forty years

The ticking of thermometers
When the sun clears out of the mist

FLOWERS

Drooping yellow and orange hawkweed,
Oxeye daisy between the pavement
And second-growth forest, while I
Was stopped consulting a map—
I didn't know where I was going
But it seemed important
To know where I was.
Either the heat or the banality
Of being without work. . .

*

Lipsticks of dawn, strangers ambling
A beach, bones of unusual fish,
Or the face emerging from under
The shadow of a pier, someone
Who could be loved if the right
Personality happened by. Myself,
For instance. . .

*

With flower boxes on fronts
Of bungalows along the way
(petunias mostly)
Until the last gas station
Was in the distance—
Frank O'Hara said, the country
Is the city without houses.

There was a time when I thought
That was insightful—
A momentary lilt to the air

*

Or that tedious hour
Awaiting daylight

*

Crouching
Before a goatsbeard flower—
Beyond me
The only bird for miles
Is attending a burdock,
A northern bird without color,
The air so dry, like everything
Might crack open. . .

TWO

TRAINS

He sat in his wool sweater,
Time passed
From the opposite ridge at night through branches,
Security lights illuminated windows of Pullmans
Ready to be refurbished. He preferred to see the cars
Clacking north to the seaweed in Ludington harbor
Where a train ferry sat—faces, men and women
Animated, en route to timbered lodges in mountains,
Drinking, carrying on—measured aggression
After seasons of being polite

SKIN

On the art museum steps
A man in a wormy cardigan sprinkled salt.
A fresh gust out of the east made Remco flinch.
I haven't eaten meat in twenty years, he confessed.
Opinions vary, I said. Wires criss-crossing above us
As we hesitated for traffic. How you like
Your condiments arranged,
Your salads, your fruit prepared—it's in the particulars
One finds intuition, he maundered. . .

Dutch poets are called Dichters, which means
Thickeners—to thicken language and experience.
Interesting, don't you think? He attempted a grin.
But his face reminded me of a puppet's, a boxy chin
Leveraging up and down. In Old English
They were called makers. . . When one considers
That all of his wives' names started with J.
(Remco's that is), you knew he was a person
Of direction, though nuts in the long run. . .
There is also the thought, a more recent one, he concluded,
Of poets as pipe fitters, connecting pipes into a maze. . .

His accent was barely visible—shadow-like,
Paint covered by another painting. He rewrapped his scarf.
Attempted to stretch his jaw. Pausing under our local high sky,
The translations are terrible, he stated,
But I'll see what I can do. Synonyms, a little makeup. . .

TREES

You can't see it, he said

There's a broken stone causeway further downstream
That connects nothing but second growth maple and ash

Standing there like a ruin of a Roman aqueduct

But the ephemera we live with now, he lamented

I studied his soft profile—we'd once played football
On opposite teams. Well, he said, spring will be up

Soon enough. Thunder and mutant lightning

Honey in the trees, or in the wind, however that saying goes

Last month, I offered, opening my hands. . .
I'm past that now, he swiftly replied, his eye blinking

He picked up his cane
Tapped a window. You can never have enough good trees

His wife sauntered onto the four-season porch
With a tiny copper-colored dog

Whose fruit picker's truck is blocking the drive?

She wore a T-shirt that read, I survived Calvinism

*

Later I saw in the paper they'd died
When a seaplane clipped their boat on a bay

In haze, I presume. On shore, among beeches,
They kept a cottage resembling a lodge

GLEN AND TOM

In whatever hotel or town
He stood on a balcony with a drink
After a long day driving in the heat

The side of his truck was missing paint
From a fire near Seney—but that was his job,
Lumber management, northern division

Years later, perched in a bar in Oregon
I remember his grey slacks,
Pockets dribbling cash from Hollywood,
One of the tallest women I'd ever met
Returning to him from the restroom

It was around that time
He was also considering a run for a seat
On the Chippewa County board of supervisors,
Just to stay cheerful

I've always admired Teddy Roosevelt
He told me in an earnest voice,
Relighting his cigar,
Talking to me like I was a small-town reporter. . .

Then added, matter-of-factly,
You must be divorced again

AFTER THE FUNERAL

There was talk of fishing, cancer,
And the stock exchange. The trick
Said Denny, is to be a contrarian,
Not many have such self-control.
I moved toward the new widow, halfway
Across, and was intercepted by Chrissie,
In jeans, just returned from Prague,
Who whispered, this is like a Fellini flick.
My wife pointed at her watch

*

Others arrived, loosening
Their clothes like theatergoers
In from the cold. Hankies and small purses.
You old trout, said Denny, pink-faced.
Doug winked without moving his mouth.
Doubles for everyone, Denny instructed,
Winging around to locate the barmaid
In her German peasant outfit, lingering
Behind the bar to finish her drink.
Denny, I said, help me push some tables
Together. . .
Let's try to be helpful, said his wife June
Tugging on his sleeve like an orphan

FRIENDS

Attentiveness is my best friend—
Being sober when he said it

Speaking low while our lines were out
Fishing deep in a slight chop

The only boat on a reservoir where there weren't
Many trees—it was cool near the border

This was October, and I'd forgotten my fleece-lined
Windbreaker. The hills were prairie, the color

Of isolation. Distances were confusing. The day
Before he'd shown me boulders with carvings

By the Chips or the Sioux when they'd passed
Through on distant migrations. . .

Though I'd have preferred to discuss
The friends we'd known living in Seattle

Or nights outside with a bottle when our horizons
Had turned cloudy. I was also chilled. . .

I enjoy living alone, he continued, well, that is,
Me and my feline—a barn cat with face scars

that gobbled down walleye heads and innards—
It makes things simpler, like clear sky, glints of water. . .

Later we drove to the hot springs to bathe,
An oasis run by Native Americans near the end

Of a sparse road that not many seemed
To know about, cottonwoods and bleached boards

He had a girlfriend there. They also cooked our fish,
Which was the custom if you shared half your catch

They say Lewis & Clark passed through in 1805—
Somewhere there nestled another boulder

With their chiseled initials. Perhaps under water

JOSEPH AT THE LAKE

She said she couldn't communicate
With me any longer, her husband
Was suspicious (after all this time),
I hunched behind sliding glass doors
The sun not on me yet but the lake
As relaxed as it gets in April

I wasn't relaxed however, I'd had dreams
Of flailing from tall ladders, over and over.
Waiting for the coffee to brew,
Smoking a light cigarette. Spotting clouds
Above mottled hardwoods as they tightened
Swiftly. The Crow tribe thought thunder
Was the voice of a great eagle, lightning
The flash of its eyes—which I'd read somewhere. . .

Then pondering a friend's recent death,
Though more about his discipline,
How he lasted as long as he did
Looking out on prairie and rock, still working
On his project, his wife informed me.
The neighbor's daffodils erect
Stretching bright yellow and white
Like on Easter cards my aunt once sent.
Willows beginning to leaf long ribbons.
I wish I had more discipline I wanted to tell her.
I was trying to recall an anecdote to offer,
I was close to one, I had a wisp of it
When the doorbell rang. Someone selling Bibles.
After that, birds stopped their incessant
Cheeping and chirping, as well as spring peepers

From the neighbor's pond. It grew eerie
Like an assassin was slinking up the lane
In dark clothes

Wind ripped everything out of the mailbox.
The last thing I saw was a snapping turtle
The size of a trash lid, poking across grass
Near rocks along the shore

THE ROAD TO WHITE CLOUD

Tumps of fish rotting
He couldn't sell

The yellow yard of a cabin

I'd gone to a party
With friends
Who slipped off
Among cypress, sometime
Before morning,
When I was rousted
To go down to his boat,
And chug up the channel,
Nauseous
Baiting hooks with
Anchovy

*

I once rowed
Across a private lake
Angling for bluegill
The cedar skiff painted
Maroon with white oars,
An easy conversation
With water

Then to a road house

*

Somewhere in Ontario
(Parry Sound,
Penetanguishene?)
Granite rounding up
Through a glassy bay,
Gulls, dragonflies,
A thin woman in a vest
At the edge of shore:
By the end of the war
We ate cats, called them
Roof rabbits

A gnarl in her accent
Her small son
Had a growth on one eye

A day or two later
I was with circus trucks
Transporting
The scent of elephants
And mud
From one farm town
To the next

*

Following arrows
To Newfoundland,
Florida, Oklahoma
And farther west

*

Sitting behind
My buddy Henry
Two locals
Were discussing
Total depravity.
We finished
Our liver and onions
And left in fog
For the wheat harvest
On the other side
Of lava-pocked hills

*

Brittle talk with myself

Morning gloam

*

Motels sag
Back into nature
Near what resembled
An abandoned flea market,
Birch returning and tamarack

Everyone grown chubby

Wild-eyed dogs
In the rears of pickups—

Your strength is your weakness,
A judge once told me
Luckily I kept my mouth shut

*

Window open, orioles flitting
Through a familiar breeze

On this two-lane
Heading to see my brother again

WHEELS

Once she insisted I was like a car
Missing its engine. She said it over and over
With various modifications

I was sitting at the next table waiting for Neesha
(only she didn't know).
Past the glass, a Xmas tree on an icy patio,
An area otherwise abandoned.
I didn't recognize either man,
Teachers perhaps at the religious college

*

A breath of snow
Brushing the window close to my cheek.
No signs of leaving.

The tavern was filling
The other said, I met her
When she was a childcare worker
In Cincinnati. I always think of trains
When I think of Cincinnati

A BOWL OF FRUIT

When I think of that room
I see the de Kooning at the end of the hall

Sometimes rain on the long windows
The tinkering of drops on the skylight

But not Yvon
Splashing scotch into a cocktail glass

Otherwise fastidious—

In retrospect
I should have asked her more

About the famous jazz guitarist
She had been engaged to

But that much was true—

Even after she bought me a pocket knife
Sheathed in velvet

Every young man needs a knife
She informed her group

But in the restaurant her friends
Eyed me like a turnip that talked—

While she was away at her office,
I tried to read

Her unfinished essay
On the vagaries of diplomacy

Reclining
On a rug of embroidered storks

The two small Rodins
Seemed misplaced

A grand piano
She didn't play

(though I did, affecting a controlled
passion

while gazing over rooftops
at carefully maintained gardens)—

I don't remember her smell

I don't recall her fingers

The last I heard she was living in Barcelona

She never did learn to cook

Now her letters are worth money

THE WATERSHED

It's like looking up
And catching someone

Sitting nude in a window

Next time it's empty
Except for side curtains

A swish of light
From a mirror on a beer truck

Otherwise, sycamores

*

Louise told me
When they chopped down

The diseased red oak
They found arrowheads

Deep in the fibers

The stream descending
Over mossy terraces of stone

Before it vacates under the lane,
A culvert angling to the river

Leaves wiggling to disengage
All through the watershed

*

A resting bottle fly
A brown thread

When you watch someone
Dying, their mouth

My cousin said,
Their mouth looks like

A chip of wood
Is missing

MIGRATING DATA

She could fossick an insult
Out of every conversation

He knew whom he meant. His neighbor's half sister

*

While he was cleaning a pail
Of perch and bluegill, assorted sizes,
An old pop tune banging through his head—
Those membranes
On which a crusty residue of anger continued to dry

First she was clothed, then naked.
He recognized a mole or two.
There was someone else in shadow
Undressing too

*

A green and sandy wind sock atop a pole, flapping
With claps

Long ribbons like spit crossing water

Leaning against a shed
The smells and breezes he'd misplaced somehow

Yellow with freckles of rust,
Open prairie now beyond the fence

*

Her thoughts at 3:00 a.m.
Of sculptures in front of the shore,
Giant paper clips bending over. . .

*

The anticipation of a road trip—
It was something like that,
With the attending deflation afterwards. . .

She licked the rim of her glass
Eyes alight, then twitched,
Sighting past his shoulder,
Having felt she'd made a mistake. . .

Grandfather's tongue
Touching the tip of his pencil
Before he bore down. . .

RAVINE

A soughing sound
Through trees and hollow

Fuddles the issue

Crude face with birdsong—

If you could paint
Your soul

It would appear
Primitive,
Frowsy

Lichen wrapped,
The north slop
Of a deer's liver—

A deep sweep of wind
Alters the landscape considerably

BURNING THE OLD DOCK

Light pulsing to shore—
Did I say this before?

Blue turns to brown
(after an earlier russet),
The moon slivers
Into trees brooding our west—

A mirror on the boat (the outboard
Rocking). A shiver of flame behind us

A light come from elsewhere—
Our faces
(If one could keep enlarging the picture. . .

Pine scent and gin)—

That undulation of air, pipe puff of air,
Over weeds,
Above the separating seawall

THREE

FLORIDA

Along the Gulf Coast:
Pelicans,
Singed meat, back sweat,
Newspapers bleached by sun and chlorine

This tablecloth reminds me
Of the gynecologist's table

My dear Sally, says her husband
Everything reminds you. . .

Or the scent of citrus.
Shadow of wistfulness.
Regret.
Dying perfume

COLORS

The favorite color that year was tan,
Some called it sand, for buying clothes
(including shoes), cars, paint for houses,
Fences, reflecting a national mood. . .

And one was thought to be a bit rough
Around the edges, or sometimes unique,
At various gatherings, if one favored black,
For example, grey, or even red. . .

Still, there was the odor of tar and metal,
Locust trees with thorns, and when the heat
Kicked up: elected malfeasance, prostitution
Among housewives, fouled drinking water. . .

By cracky, grandfather used to say.
Or when Lois said, she was lonely as a wave
And Dave said, maybe if there was only one. . .

And my brother said churches smell
Like death, and I stopped shaving everyday,
Tossed my hat, threw away my pipe and tobacco,
In short, things grew mildly roguish. . .

We were sitting by the water, watching a loon
And a wood duck swimming and diving together,
Though I kept thinking of paths in mud
Sturgeons create along bottoms of lakes. . .

And you said, before there were roads
There were canoes, just as an owl

About the size of a football passed
Close to my ear at twilight. And one tries

To imagine footpaths and long sight lines
When lower branches of trees were eighty feet up,
Only the sound of a viable paddle. We were
That earnest, the deep yellow of our lamplight. . .

THE LAKE

Dry snow, the pines scaly
As deer parade single file
As if on duty, declining
The ridge without effort
Their nostrils and breath
Suddenly enlarged, down
To the dock stacked
Under snow and
What has blown into it,
Twigs and bark from birches,
And out onto ice
Above fish staring skyward
As dry as stuffed bass and pickerel
Mounted over a mantel

Growing smaller, like in a dust
Of snowflakes,
Or a broken sentence
In Old English
During that era we did
So many illuminating detours
—a breeze stirs,
Something barks back

As the surface bends
Under its own weight

MORE STORIES

Like the smell of dog sweat
On a back seat in summer

He was so fat, she said, you could
Show movies on his rear end

*

Nearby his brothers ambled
With lunch pails over the tracks
Past the cathedral and convent,
A scent of bleach in the air

*

Humming a Sam Cooke tune
In the paint store on Fuller, the succor
Of air-conditioning on a slow afternoon
Growing hazy. Sid had promised him
Sunfish fillets from Petty's Bayou
But returned empty handed. . .
Somewhere along the coast a storm
Blossoming over dunes,
An ambush of wind, like some revelation. . .

*

He shakes his head like a comic
On stage before dancers prance in

But Gary was thinking of a hawk moth
He'd seen at a trumpet vine
The evening before

*

Claps of steam
Issuing from sewer grates,
The bickering, the kerosene,
Peach baskets stacked in the cellar

My great grandmother,
Shortly before she died,
Sharing tinted prints of snakes
Devouring a biblical family

*

Otherwise, at the bowling alley
Across the street from the antique store,
Margo, three children in college,
Has left through the back door
With five firemen after their shift,
A forest of Bud bottles behind

CICADAS IN JULY

Re Nicole Eisenman's "The Triumph of Poverty"

The sheriff's deputy leaned on the open door
Of his cruiser, I never liked your name, he said

The man seated on a log sighed—
Because of the light, the stream was salmon-colored

A short wind coughed in a branch above his head

On a nearby estate the party had stalled
After margaritas. Lights flickered every so often

The actor, once famous for tense war roles,
Jumped on a sofa. I'm Captain America

He announced, waving his arms, bouncing
From cushion to cushion. Someone began to cry

While I was looking for Miss Terpstra
With her yellow dog Plato—she was my ride—

Earlier on the veranda, the fields flowing down
From the knoll, looking like a postcard

From rural France

She had asked, what's in my hand?
I don't want to know, I replied

*

Walking back in leafy darkness, I pictured
A gentle tavern around a curve, past a glade

A sheriff's car sped by. Pebbles skittering.
Otherwise, tree frogs and crickets

Swallows and bats

I had a friend who was the only one left alive
When the enemy overran their perimeter

Thirty years later his therapist convinced him
He had been there, wounded

Lying in his bunker that night

*

Just when you believe matters are resolved

*

I had a dream an Amish buggy rode up and slipped
Over the railing of the bridge

Cars stopped, fistfights ensued.
From the window of the motel I asked my son

Now how are we going to cross?

Then everyone on the bridge ran
As if fighters and bombers were approaching over water

Like what?
Like cartoon insects, small and large respectively

When I turned my son was gone too

A LETTER

The river smells better in winter.
Otherwise, work progresses
In little grey fits.
History, said Berlin, is a series
Of disappointments. I have
Nothing to add.
They found a petrified
Shark's tooth, non-indigenous
It seems but riveting—
Indians trading eons ago.
The show was a success
In that crowds were large
And noisy. I have the flu.
Steve hasn't repaid me
The short term loan
He pleaded for. I'm tempted
To fling him, cane and all,
From the 6th Street bridge.
I'm rarely out of my pajamas
This past week, looking down
Where streetcars flourished
And everyone wore hats.
It's a memory I never owned
But it seems like one.
Before pajamas, as you know,
People wore remodeled sacks.
They were an itchy bunch.
But in those days
You could hear the drums
Long before an army appeared.
I read that hunter-gatherers

Were healthier (and taller)
Than citizens in early cities—
But they kept being drawn in.
Half-truths and sexual ticklers.
Grew jaded.
When desire disappears
It seems odd it ever occurred.
I've been feeling flattened
Myself. Watching TV.
Doodling on napkins.
Then what sprites into view,
Into consciousness,
Like an egret in summer
In Michigan, is that
I never should have taken
Advice from Roger—
I never liked puzzle boxes.
I've never been envious
Of Pauly or Frank, though
I appreciate their houses
Stacked on the river. The dog
Rolled in a dead salmon
It found in diminishing snow.
Now I'm hanging my head
Like a lamb

A WARBLE, A WAVE

Looking up, a yellowy sheen of ease
Descends from dunes

You meander a muddy track
Along water fields—
A landscape acquainted
With a good number of paintings
All saying the same thing—

Whereas dunes
Climb into a different climate

Leached bones and dry fire pits,
Basins
Where the wind has rearranged things

*

Where light shades white,
Desert beetles, desert flowers

You, like a traveler missing a map,
Raddled a bit by heat between ridges,
Unwrap a small piece of cheddar
And crouch

Among butterflies and deer flies—

At the base of a bluff
A spring trickles with winter water,
Sand sifting over shelves of peat

Attached to blackened trunks of trees,
Waterlogged, bark just separating
After nine thousand summers

TROUT OPENER

Sometimes nothing interesting happens—
The difference between youth and old age.
It was snowing in Cadillac, raining in Kalkaska

The way the stream muscled so quickly
A remembered face, a remembered torso
But it's really shit when your health goes

Said Uncle Bunny—though he wasn't my uncle,
Someone else's, someone mired in a more
Tribal family, from what I gleaned from Bunny

He threw one can out the car window
Opened another. This beer is not so cold anymore.
But as I was saying, he tapped my shoulder

You hike out behind the house, see where bucks
Have been scraping their antlers, and here
We find stakes with orange streamers

For new township sewer lines—all
The round faces of ground animals looking
For leadership, paper trash from the highway

When I was a kid we'd reach under the bank
And pull steelhead out with our hands.
The next thing I knew I was wading in fronds

Batting bullets in New Guinea. All I tried
To think about were the more interesting parts
Of Alice—along with snow, deep shafts of winter. . .

A year later he died during an operation—
His flesh inside too rotten to be tied
Back together, or so said his son, a dapper jeweler

Thin smooth hands, beagle eyes

IN THE CITY PARK

The sky grey as the sidewalks
And monuments, the YMCA converted into
Exclusive condos, I pause
On a funeral sort of day, a bit of ice
Remaining in grasses. Envisioning a pit
Without a bottom, bodies tumbling like ants—
Something from a dream while I was ill.
I'm the only one here. My trench coat is long and black
I sit on the ends of it. A detective
Without a license, much less a weapon.
Even the bars are closed. It must
Be a holiday. Or the end of the world
And I'm the only one who doesn't know,
Which would be odd. Time is tricky,
Grandmother had complained near the end.
Even the pigeons have fled

THE NEIGHBORHOOD

Fruit of Osage orange bobbing down Mears Creek
Until they lodge against rocks at the rapids

If you climb a small tree you can see the lake. . .

Lingering up the road and set back, a trading post
Is nailed shut, the one window whitewashed,
Probably full of junk. No one notices it
Behind overgrown lilacs, tall grasses. . .

Where I live south of the two-lane were cabins
Of fisherman, though none remain today
Except those incorporated into larger cottages. . .
Virgin pine and hardwoods, towering timber,
Though some have been ruined by storm and disease.
A fine quietness when wind isn't blowing over water. . .

Even further along the road alpaca graze
Throughout a pasture. One morning they were loose,
Gazing from the blacktop seemingly full of wonder.
With neighbors we managed to crowd them over
Into their enclosure before the sheriff showed up. . .

Willy told me he had a friend who helped tear
The barn apart for its lumber, and found a Civil War
Pistol wrapped tight in oilcloth. As it turns out, a soldier
Walked home from the war, then shot himself
In the head two days later, his mother sliding the gun
Between wallboards after the funeral

By this time the trading post would have evolved
Into a general store. . .

Off and on too, archeological digs have occupied
The edges of Harlow's Swamp, an area where Indigenous
Families had camped for thousands of summers. . .

Bear in mind, water levels are higher now
Because of the dam. . .

TRACKS

Sucking on cough drops
Hunched under hemlocks

Lynx tracks, martin tracks
Deer tracks, tracks of my own

Crossed tracks, moronic tracks
Bear tracks under flinty clouds

Oaks and hickory stretching
Dully—the errors in such

Stillness, as in monuments
And train tracks, squirrel

Tracks, brittle with ice
Set in snow

One grows lean

Like the last guard
On the last atoll whistling

Through crusty teeth
Tracks of ships, tracks of planes

Tracks of bugs—
Under baleful sky

Tracks of thoughts
On a rusty chain

Clanking into depths
Of unescorted hearsay

Fainter tracks of mice and voles

THREE THINGS

I. Bluestem Grasses, Sand Reed

Gouts of smoke from a car ferry
Gulls like pennants

Cross currents colliding
Scent of gasoline and ashes

Heat crackling along an inside
Water line. Rocking through

The channel in the ferry's wake
People seemed pleased on decks

Of their slight boats, waving
To fishermen dotting both piers

While on the beach, wooden remains
Of slippery slats, galled and discolored

A man said to his son, yes, there were
Pirates on the Great Lakes once

Would he mention treasure?
The boy would dig holes for years

He eyed me distrustfully. . .

So the minutes grow distracted,
A gust off water, voices from a charter

As mature cottonwoods remain

Evening primrose, pitcher's thistle,
Hairy puccoon grow near the asphalt

Just past the dented metal fence

II. In Spring

A staging area for new trailers
Fresh from the factory

An unprofitable golf course,
White boulders I first thought

Were sheep scattered on a downslope,
I was in dairy country

After a belt of burr oak, a spot of prairie,
I'd meant to stop by my nephew's house

But the road beside the river was flooded

*

Perhaps the next exit, a puzzle
Of wetlands, pines and hardwoods

Because I had leisure for the first time
In weeks. Gravel roads, sounds that magnify

Into shades of new vegetation

People who've retreated with dogs
Into lost acres. Herons and turtles. . .

All the days hanging low in vines
Adjacent to rural taverns. . .

I had the rest of the afternoon
To drive to Howard City for the affidavit

III. In the Offing

If I become too serious, tell me
To shut up. But this was a conversation

That occurred in a dream—before which
I'd been reading a newspaper, all stories

Constructed by me, though I didn't,
Of course, know it

The world tipsy,
The lake water somewhat thin

Clouds like cement bags
Tinged with rust. Beauty is relative,

Truth elusive, someone reported—
As a teenager I made it my motto

One summer I lived on panfish,
The surface of the bay, the inland

Tang of it, a pikey odor,
Cottages rheumy-eyed

Where they clot together near
The boat launch. Turkeys gliding

Over wet roofs. . .

*

One wakes to sleep dust
As droplets smear on glass

The silence of photographs
As regrets grow fuzzy

Though I won't admit to any
I didn't teach science for nothing

What comes working around the edges,
Mold and motes. Dead willows from a distance

Like enormous mushrooms. Nothing strays
But eyes

On shore, tall grasses stiff, the sun flat,
Fish rising

*

Four yellow
And six blue artificial flowers

In a vase below the window
On a dusky table, where he sat

If the wall had been painted red
It would have resembled a Matisse

MEANWHILE

Jack pine, red oak, poplar
Interspaced by fern—the occasional
Birch, maple, and white pine—one could
Picture mammoths munching through
(afraid of nothing, though that would change),
Herding up beside water
To rest and socialize

After pursuing grouse all day, without luck,
I pour a drink outside my tent, like a fictional
Character (and who isn't?)

Is everything too old or too new?

Or like an aged explorer, dropping his pack,
Who loitered here at twilight frowning,
A long way west from the arms of home—
Who may or may not
Have sensed trepidation. Covert asides,
Let's imagine

The tight rattle of leaves,
The clarity of shore water

ACKNOWLEDGMENTS

Special thanks to L. TenHarmsel, H. Meijer, D. Wakoski,
D. Gerber, A. Kleinzahler, C. Dombrowski, C. Sterry,
J. Otterbacher, G. Peterson, B. Van Dinther

ROBERT VANDERMOLEN is the author of twelve collections of poetry. He has been publishing poetry since the mid-1960s. His poems appear regularly in periodicals such as the *London Review of Books*, *Grand Street*, *Parnassus*, *Poetry*, *Epoch*, *Michigan Quarterly Review*, *Bald Ego*, and *Saint Ann's Review*. He lives and works in Grand Rapids, Michigan.

milkweed
editions

Founded as a nonprofit organization in 1980, Milkweed Editions is an independent publisher. Our mission is to identify, nurture and publish transformative literature, and build an engaged community around it.

Milkweed Editions is based in Bdé Óta Othúŋwe (Minneapolis) within Mní Sota Makhóče, the traditional homeland of the Dakhóta people. Residing here since time immemorial, Dakhóta people still call Mní Sota Makhóče home, with four federally recognized Dakhóta nations and many more Dakhóta people residing in what is now the state of Minnesota. Due to continued legacies of colonization, genocide, and forced removal, generations of Dakhóta people remain disenfranchised from their traditional homeland. Presently, Mní Sota Makhóče has become a refuge and home for many Indigenous nations and peoples, including seven federally recognized Ojibwe nations. We humbly encourage our readers to reflect upon the historical legacies held in the lands they occupy.

milkweed.org

Interior design by Mary Austin Speaker and Tijqua Daiker
Typeset in Filosofia

Filosofia was designed by Zuzana Licko
for Emigre in 1996 as a contemporary
interpretation of Bodoni.

CPSIA information can be obtained
at www.ICGtesting.com
Printed in the USA
JSHW040344110521
14583JS00002B/4